THE CATS OF IRELAND:

An Irish Gift For Cat Lovers, With Legends, Tales, & Trivia Galore

Séamus Mullarkey

Plain Scribes Press

The Cats Of Ireland:

An Irish Gift For Cat Lovers, With Legends, Tales, And Trivia Galore!

Plain Scribes Press

www.plainscribespress.com

Paperback: 978-1-7367630-0-1

WHY NOT GET A **FREE E-BOOK** TO FIND OUT IF YOUR CAT MIGHT ACTUALLY BE IRISH…?

Making a connection with others around the world is the best part of writing. From time to time, I send emails with details of new releases, special offers, and other news related to books about Irish topics, cats, and to humor in general.

If you sign up for my mailing list today, I'll send you a wee e-book that outlines the twenty-five signs that your cat is Irish.

You can get this e-book **for free**! As a **special bonus** you'll **also** be able to get free copies of my future books—all just for giving your honest review! Simply use the link or scan the code below.

https://bit.ly/3kian13

To Frankie and Charlotte, and to John who brought them into our lives…

Time spent with cats is never wasted.

—Sigmund Freud

This book is dedicated to my niece Éabha Slattery, a highly intelligent young lady from Galway who loves cats, and to the much-missed Mary Gibney, the greatest cat sitter of all time....

Acknowledgements

Thanks to Roger for his unparalleled skills as an editor and as a collaborator who is enamored of, and knowledgeable about, all things feline. Thanks also to Cat O'Connell for her role as trusted collaborator and as a fellow cat nut.

Preface

Thank you sincerely for buying this book. I'm pleased it caught your attention and that you've decided to add it to your bookshelf. I've long had a fascination with cats as well as with my own Irish culture, having found strength and entertainment in both. A couple of years ago, I realized that--in my distinctively rambling, long-winded way--I could meld these two passions into what I hoped would be an entertaining little volume. So, I eventually got around to writing it, and here it is...

Again, thanks so much. Happy reading!

Séamus Mullarkey, February 2021

Contents

Introduction

On the Emerald Isle, life traditionally revolved around both the hearth, the warm focus of everyday life, and the barn, which was home to both precious livestock and the harvested crops which would feed the farmer and his brood over the chilly, wind-lashed winter months. Unfortunately, the barn also attracted miscellaneous wee vermin in the form of mice and rats. It was in precisely this context that our fuzzy feline pals proved most useful to the farming communities where they lay their whiskered heads, providing their farmer friends with an invaluable defense against those insidious rodents.

Meanwhile, indoors in the space where people dwelled, life revolved around the all-important toasty hearth. Here, tended with care both day and night throughout the year, a warm and luminous peat fire provided a place from whence ensued not only a glow but also provided the means with which to cook and to dry goods of all sorts, whether they be foodstuffs, rain-sodden items of clothing, or blankets and bedding in need of an airing from the damp climate. This flaming hub was also the center of the legendary Irish hospitality. It was therefore a privileged spot to occupy. In this famously welcoming culture, it was standard practice to reserve the location closest to the toasty fire for any visitors who might happen by. It's no wonder then that you'd often find a dozing kitty claiming this spot of honor. You see, a cat's place on the traditional Irish homestead alternated between the blazing peat fire and the mouse-filled confines of the barn.

Fast forward to the Ireland of today, in which many inhabitants work in the tech industry rather than on traditional agricultural land holdings, and you're likely to spot the same pattern. The modern tabby will still alternate between a shed or other outbuilding and a cozy spot at the heart of the family, be it fueled by peat, firewood, or the clean blue flame of natural gas. And although some outward details may have changed, the pattern remains as constant as the bond between the Irish and their beloved, barely domesticated feline pals. Cats are continuing to increase in popularity as a domestic companion. Currently, that bond is only getting stronger by the day, and according to a recent survey, cat owners across the Republic testify that their cats really "get them," perhaps even more so than those around them in the human realm!

So, on to the business at hand! I now present to you a host of quirky, entertaining, and altogether absorbing tales of the feline denizens of Ireland. I dearly hope this modest collection of cute kitties and the Irishmen and Irishwomen who adore them tickles your whiskers. I pray to the cat gods that you derive as much enjoyment from reading this tome as I did pawing through the research, scratching out the words and grooming the feline-focused prose. This book may not be purrrrfect, but it is my sincere wish that you do in fact find it to be the cat's meow.

Cats in History

Long, Long Ago

The history of the domestic cat in Ireland is fuzzy or should that be furry—sorry, we couldn't resist the play on words! Evidence exists, however, that wild cats roamed the verdant hills and valleys of Ireland well before the arrival of the ordinary housecat, *Felis catus*. However, we should clarify that these wild cats died out and that they are not the ancestors of our current-day domestic kitty. It hasn't been possible to pinpoint the arrival of the domestic cat on Irish shores, but each wave of settler and invader alike almost certainly brought with them a new crop of kitties. As in other civilizations, there is a close correlation between the tantalizing bounty of the grain harvest and our furry friends "volunteering" to keep the accompanying hungry rodents in check. Evidence for this can be spotted at archaeological excavations in some medieval settlements. In one instance, at Ballyvass in County Kildare, archaeologists came upon the skeleton of a cat near a kiln where the ancient Irish dried cereal. This resting place by the oven that dried the grain was presumably located at the heart of a bountiful hunting ground for that intrepid tabby from oh-so-long ago.

Irish Cat Names

What's in a name? If it's your cat's name we're talking about, the answer might be "rather a lot." There is a whole array of factors to consider when bestowing a moniker on your favorite fluffster. We're particularly taken with two of the oldest Irish cat names (found in medieval Irish law texts), *Méone*, a diminutive meaning 'little meow', as well as *Cruibne*, meaning 'tiny paws.' Of course, you could name your cat after your favorite Irish pop star; Bono, Enya, and Sinead all spring to mind. You might also go for names common among the human population of Ireland. We're thinking of the good old reliables like Jack or Paddy. Or you could choose Eileen or Kathleen for the female kittens. Then, of course, you could match your pet's personality to a key purr-sonality trait, such as *whiskey* for a little party monster or *craic* (meaning great fun) for the one who keeps you in fits of laughter all the time. Finally, you could use your pet's color as a guide. What about Dubh (meaning black, pronounced "dove") or Bán (meaning white, pronounced "bawn")? However, the more cynical amongst you might think it doesn't really matter anyway since our darling cats rarely come when they're called—except when there are delicious cat treats involved—in which case they don't care what you call them!

Viking Cats

From the eighth to the eleventh centuries, the predatory Vikings set out from their homes and fjords in Scandinavia to pillage and conquer Ireland and other parts of Europe. These fearsome raiders were known for their bloodthirsty ways as well as their rapacious greed for valuable goods, especially precious artifacts such as those jeweled chalices in Ireland's churches and monasteries. Indeed, the very mention of the Vikings shook terror in the Irish heart. Yet, over time the Vikings settled among Ireland's population and were in fact the founders of Ireland's capital city of Dublin and played a large role in Irish life. Since we are talking about Vikings in a book of feline facts, you won't be surprised to learn that cats played an integral part in the Viking culture. Thor, the god of Thunder tried to prove his power by lifting a giant cat, but poor old Thor could only raise one of the mighty creature's paws. It shows you just who was most powerful in Viking mythology! Felines always have the upper hand. In addition, Freya, the goddess of fertility, rode in a chariot pulled by gigantic cats, which were themselves a symbol of fruitfulness—perhaps an allusion to the fact that cats reproduce so rapidly (in one year, a healthy female cat can birth three litters, bringing an annual average of twelve kittens into the world!)

An Irish Witch and Her Cat

Since the misty dawn of recorded time, cats have been known as aides and confidantes to witches. Such companions to witches, whether cats or other creatures, were known as familiars and they were supposed to aid the witches with their magic. It was perhaps their nearly supernatural grace and air of mystery that made cats so suitable for this role.

Unfortunately, both cats and their witchy owners were horribly persecuted for sorcery during the witch trials that swept Europe in the Middle Ages. However, it turns out that the luck of the Irish was real for the feline familiars. While in many other parts of Europe women who were guilty of no more than a little traditional medicine and an unwillingness to fit in to the roles assigned them by the patriarchy were hung or burned for witchcraft, Ireland had relatively few witch trials, making it a safer place for witches' cats than other European countries. However, that is not to say that there was no persecution of witches in Ireland. The victim of the first recorded witch trial in Ireland, was named Dame Alice Kyteler. Born in 1280, Alice came from a wealthy Kilkenny family. It was the illness of husband number four (after the suspicious deaths of hubbies one through three…) that brought her to the attention of the authorities. Insistent inquisitors tried to pin the rap on Alice, but despite the (torture induced) claims of her maid that Alice consorted with all manner of devilish spirits, including having a cat as a familiar, it seems Alice had nine lives! You see, despite being sentenced to burn at the stake, Alice managed to escape, not on the flying broomstick her maid accused her of riding, but with the help of her aptly named brother-in-law Roger Outlawe. Rumor has it she fled to England, and while no record survives about whether or not she found new kitty companions after she sailed to safety, we like to hope she brought a little magic into her new life in the form of a black cat or two to make her new domicile feel like the Irish home she had to flee.

Irish Medieval Cat Laws

A society's system of rules provides significant insight into what it prioritizes and holds dear. Scholars have long been intrigued by the Medieval Irish laws regarding cats. Yes, you heard that correctly: the Medieval Irish had an entire body of law that related to our furry friends. It was known as the *Catslechtae*. This shows that the Irish at the time valued felines—and for reasons that would not be unfamiliar to the modern cat lover. First, the medieval Irish wisely recognized the monetary value of a cat's ability to kill rodents, asserting that an excellent mouser was valued at the same amount as three milk cows. This valuation is extraordinary when you think of it. Dairy herds would have been essential for dietary and hence for economic reasons. Even more impressive is that the Irish valued cats not only for their capacity to keep rodents at bay, but they also appreciated the marvelous ability that cats have to comfort and soothe. We're talking about nothing other than the cat's ability to purr. A cat who could not purr or didn't purr satisfactorily was valued at only half the monetary amount that his purring equivalent would be. It's amazing how prescient this was since scientists today theorize that the frequency of a cat's purr helps enhance healing in humans. Unfortunately, the picture painted by cat law wasn't entirely rosy. There was mention of the downside of the cat's crafty nature. For example, guidelines were set down which specified how much was to be paid to people whose food was stolen by cats! In addition, courts levied fines when cats defecated in unacceptable places such as on the floor of a dwelling place. Bad kitty!

Carson's Orange Cat

Sir Edward Carson was a prominent Unionist politician of the early 20th century. He and his fellow Loyalists were staunchly attached to the British crown. They fiercely opposed any lessening of Britain's ties with Ireland. Orange is the traditional color of the Unionist community and one of Carson's compatriots composed a ditty imagining the reaction of Carson's Orange Cat to the prospect of surrendering to the Irish nationalist cause. In the songwriter's imaginings, the cat is just as staunchly opposed to the possibility as Carson himself. Here are a few lines from the lyrics in which the fierce, pro-British feline vehemently expresses his political sentiments:

Sir Edward Carson has a cat
It sits upon the fender,
And every time a mouse it gets
It shouts out "No Surrender!"

Glamourpusses

Irish Instagram Stars

Most modern men and women might agree that social media seems to have taken over our lives. We just can't help ourselves, chronicling nearly every aspect of our daily human existence. And, when that doesn't yield enough shareable online content, we resort to chronicling our cats. Who hasn't whiled away a good part of an afternoon or evening browsing through images of cute kitties? Hands up--and be honest now! Well, Ireland is no exception to the rule. There are quite a number of Irish cats making their impact on the Internet. And sure, why wouldn't they? Aren't Irish people—and by logical extension Irish cats—among the most interesting, sociable, and fascinating types you're likely to come across? If you're wondering whom to follow, some of the cats below are possible contenders for your next feline bookmark. First stop are our personal favorites. These include kitty and JJ who go by the handle @kittyinthecity1. These two are rescue cats, one white and one black and white. One of their favorite pastimes is getting tangled up in shopping bags. They are the ultimate feline shopaholics! Next stop is @rivercottagecattery. This channel is for those who need variety and the ultimate fix of cuteness overload. Here you can feast your eyes on cats who are staying at the cattery while their owners are away.

Hooray for Hollywood!

Now you might be forgiven for wondering what on earth the connection could be between Irish cats and the world capital of the entertainment industry all the way on the other side of the globe—in Hollywood, California. Well, the link starts early on—all the way back in the silent film era. Matt Moore was one of three brothers from County Meath, all of whom sought fame and fortune as silent film actors. During a long and active career, Matt Moore made 221 movies between 1912 and 1958. This Irish thespian was cat crazy and well known for bringing his pets on the set. Matt even persuaded directors to let his kitties play roles in the movies! Moore himself has a star on the Hollywood Walk of Fame, but his kitty companions aren't lacking for recognition. Two of his cats also have stars on the animal portion of the very same fabled stretch of sidewalk.

It may surprise you to know that Ireland's cats continue to play a role in Hollywood. In picturesque Rathangan, County Kildare, Mary Owens and Rita Moloney run Fircroft Animal Casting; they have been training and handling cats (and other animals) for TV and movie work for over thirty years now. If anyone can get a cat to do what it's told it's these two intrepid Irish ladies!

Enya's Castle Full of Cats

Enya's otherworldly and enchanting melodies have won the Donegal-born songstress Grammy, Oscar, and Golden Globe nominations, and gleaned her numerous other prestigious awards and even an honorary degree from NUI Galway. Like her ethereal music, Enya's public persona is mysterious, lovely, and somehow not of this realm. It's not any wonder then that her private life is equally steeped in mystery. Despite the ubiquity of her songs like Orinoco Flow, we know little about this cherished chanteuse. "She keeps herself to herself," as the Irish would put it. However, we do know a few intriguing tidbits. For one, she lives in an imposing Victorian Castle next door to Bono. This secure retreat from the world is surrounded by hefty 9-foot-thick stone walls, topped in turn by 4 ft railings in some sections. This lady isn't alone in her fortress, however. She shares her vast, impenetrable dwelling with a menagerie of up to a dozen cats. The lady has taste after all! We presume that she spends her days in the company of her beloved felines composing and rehearsing her beguiling melodies. Whatever the day-to-day realities of her reclusive life one thing is for sure--she's one of the most captivating yet elusive cat ladies on the planet. We just hope that one day she releases an album with her kitties as backup singers…

Adventurous Cats

The First Irish Cat in a Hot-Air Balloon

In 1784, just over a year after the first human-crewed balloon flight made by the Montgolfier brothers in France, an Irish engineer by the name of Richard Crosbie experimented with what he called an "aeronautic chariot," or what you or I might dub a hot-air balloon.

A born showman, Crosbie sent a cat in a balloon from Dublin to the Isle of Man (halfway between Ireland and England). On its journey, the balloon toppled into the sea and the poor (doubtlessly terrified) kitty was lucky enough to be rescued by a passing ship. Nowadays, ballooning remains popular in Ireland with Irish Balloon Flights offering trips over spectacular sights such as the Boyne Valley and Trim Castle. Ireland is also the site of some important hot-balloon championships. However, we're pretty confident that few cats have taken part in recent years. They've probably heard what happened to their unfortunate predecessor!

Traveling Far and Wide

While our furry feline friends have spread to all corners of the globe, most domestic cats are precisely that: domestic, with no particular inclination to stray far from the comforts of home. Why would they? Lords and ladies of their domain, their home turf is their manor house, with everything suited to their needs. And long may they rule over it! However, whether through luck or other circumstances, some Irish cats have roamed far and wide. Sometimes, the journey resulted from their owner's wanderings. Take, for instance, the case of George, an adorable orange male tabby. He and his Irish-born owner Fiona had lived a contented life in Sydney, Australia. Then, due to ill health, Fiona had to return home to Ireland. At this point she entrusted her darling pet to what she thought was a trustworthy neighbor. Fiona's plan was to return to Australia at a later date and take the kitty back to Erin's shores with her. Unfortunately, the neighbor moved away and left poor George to his own devices. He became a stray and ended up being taken by a kindly soul to a vet's office over 10 miles away. There, his microchip established who he was, and the vet contacted Fiona in Ireland. She realized then that she had to get her beloved George back by her side, so she started a Facebook campaign dubbed "Bring George Home." Cat lovers across the Internet opened their hearts and their wallets, and generous donations soon accumulated. Now George is back with Fiona where we're told he never stops purring.

Sticking with Australia, there's the case of Ozzie, the Sydney cat who turned up in Northern Ireland. He was taken to a Northern Irish vet who was shocked to learn from the cat's microchip that the kitty was from Sydney and that his original name was Tigger. The chip also showed that a vet had examined him in London. It seems Ozzie's owner took him to London from Australia and that from there he somehow made his way across the Irish Sea to Northern Ireland. Once it was realized that Ozzie was from Down Under, an international search was launched to reunite him with his owners. It turned out that they had spent time in London and in Northern Ireland, and it was in Northern Ireland that he ran away and could not be found. Sadly, since the search was launched Ozzie the Aussie had developed kidney problems and had to be put to sleep before he could be reunited with his owners back in the land of Oz. Devastated that they couldn't get to him in time his heartbroken asked that his ashes be sent from Ireland back to Sydney where he could rest in peace in his home country.

Pussy Went to Sea

In the chilly days of early February 2017 an entertaining episode occurred involving a sea-faring cat and one deeply surprised seafarer. Patrick, a fisherman, set off from the port of Galway as he usually did, with his mind on a lucrative day of lobster fishing. Once Patrick threw the pots into the sea, it surprised him to find a gray striped cat on board his vessel. The poor creature—who had apparently crept on board in search of tasty, fishy tidbits or perhaps an interesting place to nap, was startled awake and promptly leaped into the sea! Thankfully, the courageous Patrick skillfully rescued the soggy moggy and set off back to shore, no doubt accompanied by piteous yowls. Once in port, Patrick entrusted the by-now dry kitty to the care of the local vet who dubbed the poor mite Uisce—fittingly enough—for that's the Irish Gaelic word for water. Hopefully, Uisce has learned a lesson and won't head out for another aquatic adventure any time soon. Maybe scavenging along the docks for some scraps would be acceptable though. After all, we still want the poor old cat to have some fun...

The Blind Mountaineering Cat

The highest mountain in all of Ireland is Carrauntoohil, which reaches a height of 3,406 feet. So, it was with great interest that we learned of a 2016 ascent by Mr. Patrick Carr and his blind cat Stevie. They climbed to raise money for animal charities and to highlight how special all cats are, even if they have a physical handicap. The climb took about four hours. Stevie made the journey while alternating between walking on a leash and perching on his owner's back. As the old Irish saying goes, "Two people shorten the road." We're immensely proud of Patrick and Stevie's notable accomplishment. We wonder where they ventured next.

Lindbergh and His Lil' Kitty In The Sky

Did you know that when Charles Lindbergh took his famous first transatlantic flight he wasn't alone in that tiny cockpit? His mammoth thirty-three-and-a-half-hour flight was less lonely than you might have thought. You see by his side proudly sat a Felix the cat doll. Apart from being an immensely popular cartoon character at the time, Felix the cat was also the unofficial mascot of Lindbergh's aeronautic company. We know that the very first European country Lindbergh flew over was our own dear Ireland, though we are not sure if he propped up Felix to get a look at the Emerald Isle below. Perhaps Lindbergh brought this inanimate substitute to stand in for Patsy, his real-life pussy cat. While this intrepid tabby often flew with Charles Lindbergh, the groundbreaking pilot decided against bringing his feline friend along on the first flight to cross the Atlantic. Lindbergh, the ever-devoted cat lover, is supposed to have said: "It's too dangerous a journey to risk a cat's life." Still, he did risk his own life, proving perhaps that cats are worth far more than mere humans, no matter how famous a figure the human might be.

Song, Story, and Verse

Irish Drinking Songs for Cat Lovers

Close your eyes for a moment and imagine this scene. You're sat at the pub alongside your beloved tabby—as you might be, say on a Wednesday afternoon in late autumn. The air around you crackles with the lively conversation that the Irish are famous for. You're sipping a neat whiskey (Irish, naturally, spelled with an -ey if you please). Your dearest fluffy friend. is enjoying a saucer of artisanal catnip beer. Suddenly, your slightly soused self is overcome with a desire to burst into song. The usual Irish ditties spring immediately to mind, of course. It would be hard to go wrong with the ubiquitous "Danny Boy." Perhaps the afternoon calls for something mournful like "The Fields of Athenry" or even a rousing round of "Carrickfergus" to get the whole pub to join you in a chorus of raucous melody.

Yet, before you can part your whiskey-wetted lips to sing the first note, you catch your cat's eye and are overcome by sorrow at the thought that none of your favored melodies will have anything to do with the (nine) life experience of your kitty companion. The traditional Irish songs we all treasure contain no mention of mice or chasing one's tail, for example. If only some Irish drinking songs were related to cats. Well, there are some! Did you know that a wickedly clever fellow by the name of Marc Gunn has produced an album for just such an auditory occasion? If cat songs are what you crave, feast your ears upon "Irish Drinking Songs for Cat Lovers." Just Google it, we promise you that it's a hoot. This gifted composer even penned a song parodying that all-time classic "Whiskey in the Jar." This tongue-in-cheek re-working of that classic is, of course, titled "Whiskers in the Jar." The generous song-meister has even been kind enough to allow cat lovers to use his tunes to score cute videos of their precious kitties. So, fire up that phone and get to filming! The Internet was made for cat videos and if you play your cards right, your feline could find fame on the world wide web, all accompanied by some hilarious Irish cat songs.

Gaelic Cats

There's nothing more agreeable than the sound of Ireland's ancient Celtic tongue, Irish Gaelic. Still spoken daily by about 5% of the population and mandatory on the Irish school curriculum, this linguistic treasure holds a special place in many hearts. Next to Latin, Irish Gaelic is the European language with the longest continuous history. Recent years have seen the rise of a great deal of Irish language TV and radio programs. In addition, this complex, musical tongue lends itself easily to poetry and figurative speech, in which the Irish are unmatched. If you have an interest in things Irish—and we assume you do if you're reading this book—you might be interested in trying out some of the following phrases on your cat:

- Bi ciuin (b q win)—be quiet.
- Ná bi dána (naw b daw-nah) don't be naughty.
- Ná bac leis an cat siuid (naw bok lesh an caught shoe-ed) Don't mess with that cat over there.
- Le do thoil (leh duh hull) *Please...*

And as your cat inevitably wanders away, ignoring you disdainfully:

- Slán agat go foil mo grá (slawn ugut guh fowil mcgraw)
  Goodbye for now my love.

Raining Cats and Dogs

If you've ever been to Ireland, you'll readily testify that it rains a lot. This climatic quirk is due to its location at the edge of the Atlantic and the prevailing winds which blow across the wind-tossed seas. You've also heard the expression, "It's raining cats and dogs." Perhaps you've wondered where the phrase originates. Some have theorized that this ubiquitous phrase could have come from the Greek saying *cata doxa*, which can be translated as "contrary to experience." So, raining *cata doxa* might mean it's raining so hard you've never seen anything like it. Another explanation is that sensible cats and dogs used to shelter in thatched roofs during heavy downpours and when the torrent got intense, they'd be washed out and "rain" to the ground around the cottage. However, the correct explanation might have a more morbid origin, coming from none other than Ireland's legendary Dean Swift (the author of Gulliver's Travels). Swift wrote a poem, "City Shower" in 1710 that described floods leaving dead animals in the streets, which may have led to those who read his work relating the weather as— drumroll please—raining so hard there were dead cats and dogs everywhere—shortened to "raining cats and dogs." As Swift so skillfully put it:

> Sweeping from butcher's stall, dung, guts, and blood,
>
> Drown'd puppies, stinking sprats, all drenched in mud,
>
> Dead cats and turnip tops, come tumbling down the flood.

Kilkenny Cats

Kilkenny is a town located almost in the center of the country and its medieval streets are sure to charm even the most jaded of visitors. There's an Irish expression which says to "fight like Kilkenny cats," and the local sports team are called the Kilkenny Cats. It's a strange saying and we wondered what the origin might be. Well, we trembled upon hearing the answer. In the past, cruel British soldiers garrisoned outside the town were known to tie together cats' tails in order to have the brutal pleasure of watching the poor cats fight each other. Although many Irish sayings are charming this is one expression we wish we'd never heard...

Pangur Bán

The tale of Pangur Bán is one of the most touching stories ever told about a cat. An Irish monk in the ninth century in Carinthia, Austria was tasked with reproducing the beautiful calligraphy of a copy of St. Paul's Epistles. There would have been a whole network of Irish-founded monasteries and churches throughout Europe at this stage, a time when Ireland was known as the "Land of Saints and Scholars" for the missionary and educational work that its religious orders performed across Europe. The cat was often the only animal allowed in convents and monasteries. Authorities regarded these self-sufficient felines as the only pet animal that would not be overly distracting from a contemplative life. Also, they considered cats useful in protecting the Holy Eucharist from vermin. Well, anyhow a particular monk was toiling away into the wee hours, kept company by his cat Pangur (a popular cat's name at the time) who was designated Bán, which is the Irish Gaelic word for white. Perhaps bored witless by the repetitive task of copying the manuscript letter by letter—remember that this was in the days before the printing press when manuscripts had to be tediously copied by hand—he composed a poem in the margins of the holy book dedicated to his beloved feline companion. In skillful rhyme (and written in his native Irish tongue—perhaps because he was missing his homeland) he affectionately compares his cat hunting mice with his own hunting of words.

> *Pangur, white Pangur, How happy we are*
> *Alone together, scholar and cat*
> *Each has his own work to do daily;*
> *For you it is hunting, for me study.*
> *Your shining eye watches the wall;*
> *My feeble eye is fixed on a book.*
> *You rejoice, when your claws entrap a mouse;*
> *I rejoice when my mind fathoms a problem.*
> *Pleased with his own art, neither hinders the other;*
> *Thus we live ever without tedium and envy.*

Irish Proverbs About Cats

Irish sayings are well known for their common sense, evoking homespun wisdom with a skillful turn of phrase and an often-accurate representation of life's ups and downs. So, it's hardly surprising then that Irish proverbs relating to cats are wry and likely to raise a smile. For instance, perhaps the best known of all feline proverbs—and some people are not even aware that it is of Irish origin—is the saying "don't trust anybody who doesn't like cats." Of course, we wholeheartedly agree with that sentiment. Another interesting proverb derived from Irish Gaelic is that "the cat purrs only for the good of himself," perhaps alluding to the self-centered and willful nature of the cat. Then there's the saying "what would the son of a cat do but kill a mouse?" This is the equivalent of saying "like father like son." If your cat has had kittens, you might be able to attest to the truth of this proverb.

U2's Feline Love Song

Renowned throughout the world as emblematic of Ireland's musical genius, U2 hold a special place in the pantheon of Rock gods. One of their more unusual songs is titled *An Cat Dubh* or "the black cat" in Gaelic. This evocative song deals with the tortured angst arising from a love affair that lead singer Bono had when on a break from his then-girlfriend (and now wife). The lyrics tell us of a black cat who plays with, kills, and then sleeps beside a bird. There is some complicated imagery going on here, but the band members tell us it's about intense sexuality and who are we to disagree? *An Cat Dubh* is one of those intriguing footnotes in Rock history. And it would be about a cat. Just about everything is when you think of it!

The President's Cat

Care to join an adorable orange tabby on an exciting adventure as he travels around Ireland, visiting some of the country's most beloved landmarks? Look no further than *The President's Cat*. Written and

27

illustrated by Peter Donnelly, this children's picture book tracks the travels of the wee feline after he's accidentally left behind in Kerry when his kindly, yet forgetful, presidential owner returns from his holidays. Plenty of amiable Irish folk help kitty make his way back home to the presidential residence, Áras an Uachtaráin. The lovely illustrations feature such landmarks as the Rock of Cashel, Dublin Zoo, and Glendalough through the eyes of one brave little moggie. If your wee one is fond of cats and you'd like to introduce them to the beauty Ireland has to offer, you'd be hard-pressed to do better than this award-winning tome.

Furballs in Folklore

A Cat's Place by the Fire

Famously, Ireland's climate tends toward the damp and windy. Therefore, as previously mentioned, a toasty spot near a blazing peat fire is a coveted prize. Indeed, there's a delightful Irish folk tale which tells of the struggle between a clever cat and a dopey dog to determine who would acquire this cherished vantage point where they could warm themselves by the flames as well as keep an eye on the household. The dispute was going nowhere, so the cat suggested to the dog that they could have a five-mile race and whoever won the race would forever henceforth occupy that coveted place by the fire. The dog amiably agreed, and so, our two friends set off with the enthusiastic dog quickly overtaking the crafty kitty. However, along the way the dog came across a tramp who beat him with a stick. Understandably, the dog took a break from the competition to chase the nasty man and try to bite him. In the meantime, the tabby wound its way back home, and to that cozy spot at the fire—a position from which the "cute hoor" has never since stirred. This delightfully warm spot is his by right as it was won fair and square in this legendary competition.

The Cave of the Cats

In Rathcrogan in County Roscommon lies a seemingly innocuous cave with a triangular opening almost hidden by a thorn bush. This unassuming cave is in fact one part of a more extensive system of ring forts, holy wells, standing stones and several caves, which date back to Neolithic times, about 6,000 years ago. A 10th-century tale recounts how the famous Irish warrior Cuchulainn and two companions spent time here—in an initiation ceremony during which several terrifying cats tested their nerve. Legend has it that that *Uaimh na gCait*, its name in Gaelic or *Cave of the Cats* in English, is the fabled portal through which one might access the Irish Otherworld and the domain of the Morrigan, the Celtic goddess of battle and strife. However, entering the cave is not to be taken lightly. It's a cramped and muddy place and it's said that those daring to enter may encounter all kinds of fearful noises and apparitions, including the unearthly feline wailing from which the cave takes its name. When we visited, we couldn't be certain if we heard any cat-like noises or not, but it was an eerie experience in which one could imagine all kinds of ghostly goings-on occurring. The cave has been visited extensively over the years by many a fearless Irishman and none other than Ireland's first president, Douglas Hyde carved his name there. We're not sure if we should be happy that Hyde left a piece of history in his wake or if we should be concerned that he might have set a bad example in terms of inscribing graffiti at ancient sites of major significance. In another point of interest there are scratches which a few uninformed tourists proposed were scratches made by the infamous cave-dwelling cats. However, experts tell us that these marks are in fact an inscription in the ancient Celtic writing system called Ogham and that it reads "Fraech, …son of Medb," almost certainly referring to a renowned noble West of Ireland fighter. This indeed does lend weight to the belief that this was the site of warrior initiations.

Belfast's Castle of Nine Cats

Belfast Castle is an imposing structure with a notable feline connection. This edifice is set on a promontory that overlooks the fair city. There has been a fortified structure here since the 12th century, perched on the bluff known as Cave Hill. The current structure dates from the 19th century and is an elegant, sturdy building of architectural distinction that is rented out for events and special occasions. Legend has it that the building would enjoy good luck as long as a white cat was in residence. Paying homage to this tradition, there are nine cats in various formats enhancing the décor. These nine design elements represent the nine lives of our furry friends and are scattered throughout the premises including a cat in mosaic form as well as one in sculpture.

Cat Superstitions on Land and at Sea

Considering their mystical air, it's no wonder that there are several Irish superstitions connected with our fine feline friends. First, there's the stern admonition that killing a cat will bring a person seventeen years of bad luck. Then there's the prediction that if you dislike cats you will be carried to the cemetery in the rain. Sticking with the ailurophobic (cat-hating) connection to bad weather, there's the belief that if you mistreat cats, you will have rain showers at your wedding. As befits a sea-going nation, there are several superstitions concerning cats and the deep blue yonder. Irish sailors traditionally supposed cats to possess supernatural strengths that would protect vessels from dangerous weather. To make extra sure that their husbands' ships would be safe from the stormy seas, fishermen's wives would keep black cats at home in the hope that they would bring good luck to the men on the high seas. Another, even more extraordinary, superstition was that cats could start a gale through magic stored in their tails. That's what we'd call a tall tale about tails!

Celtic Cats

Much of Irish culture derives from the ancient Celtic world. This enigmatic and spiritual tradition still influences everyday Irish life. Given all you've learned so far, it should be no surprise that the Celts had a particular regard for cats. These regal felines were intricately linked to their most important goddess, Brigid. Cats also held a special place in the Celts' everyday affection and were practically regarded as family members. The Celts appreciated many aspects of the feline spirit including their delicate ways and their intuitive sensitivity. In fact, cats were held up as an example to follow. What's more, cats were directly linked to magical powers. Consequently, the Druids considered cats an important link between this world and the other world, a connection they believed was extraordinarily strong and that influenced every aspect of their daily lives.

The Little White Cat

If a tale chock full of Irish adventure and magic featuring a crafty little cat is what you seek, look no further than "The Little White Cat," written by Edmond Leamy in his book, *Irish Fairy Tales*. This sprawling tale features the plucky Princess Eileen, captured (as fairy tale princesses are wont to be) by the dastardly giant Trencross. Trapped in his great, well-nigh impenetrable castle, she despairs of escaping the horrible fate of marriage to a murderous brute. That is, until a curious little white cat visits her and kicks off a rollicking tale of adventure. This matchmaking little moggie also finds his way to the dashing Prince of the Silver River and sets our hero and heroine upon a series of typically mystifying tasks (balls of fairy dew are involved). After some secrets are revealed, journeys are taken, and a spot of amnesia is overcome, our hero and heroine of course earn their happily-ever-after, to the apparent delight of the little white cat (who turns out to be feline royalty in his own right). The tale itself has many more twists and turns than I've shared here, but if you're a parsimonious bibliophile, you're in luck! This book is in the public domain, so a quick search of the Internet should yield you a free copy to peruse at your leisure.

King of the Cats

Sure, we've all seen our precious moggies indulge in a spot of goofy behavior or feral-like fun, but there also resides in most cats a profound dignity, a regal bearing one might say (when one hasn't just witnessed one's cat grooming their nether regions with gusto). This inherently aristocratic spirit leads many a cat owner to give our companions the royal treatment, granting all due deference to the fuzzy sovereign who rules all that they survey (even if their kingdom consists of only a modest studio apartment). But while your Princess may certainly deserve to be treated like a queen, there can only be one true King of the Cats, at least according to one popular Irish folktale.

In this story, a man from Cork foolishly ignores the long-honored tradition followed by his superstitious neighbors. While they insist that offering one bowl of milk a week to the *Cat Sith* (King of the Cats) is the key to keeping the spirits happy, this old man doesn't just neglect to respectfully offer a delectable dairy treat, he actually poisons the bowl he sets outside his door. Sure enough, before long he finds a black cat with a white chest (traditional coloring for cat royalty, it seems) dying on the front step, and this awful fellow heads to the local pub to discover who the owner of this poor, poisoned puss might be. The fool brags to his fellow drinkers about what he's done, and the pub cat, having heard the tale, proclaims "that must make me the new King of the Cats!" In an act of revenge, or perhaps just solidarity with his feline brethren, this newly crowned kitty attacks the awful old man, chasing him out of town, and the wretched cat killer is never seen or heard from again!

Other-Worldly Cats

Halloween Cats

Halloween is a mystical night shrouded in swirling mists and beguiling mysteries. We're not sure if you know of the Celtic roots of this festival. In its original form, the special day was known as Samhain. This occasion was the night between October 31st and November 1st and marked the end of the harvest season. As the nights were getting longer, and the light was getting shorter and dimmer, the ancient Irish saw this as a period of introspection. They also regarded this autumn evening as a time when the veil between the different spheres, that of our world and the next world became thinner. During this lessening of the demarcation, spirits were said to be able to drift through more easily from one side to the other, lending the whole holiday an ethereal air. Cats, with their mystical aura, have always given the impression they have one paw in this world and one paw in the other dimension. Besides, they can see better in the dark than humans, although the common misconception that they can see as well as in the daytime is a myth. However, it is true that their sense of hearing is acute, with powers of auditory observation extending to frequencies that mere humans (with their lowly fur-free ears) can't detect. Perhaps it is this overdeveloped aural capacity that would allow cats to hear murmurings from the beyond. Therefore, it's only logical that we strongly associate them with this holiday of Halloween. Being messengers between the dimensions, it makes sense to treat them well. In recognition of this fact the Irish often left out an extra special saucer of milk on this holiday.

My Cat's Curse Upon You

Anyone who's ever met even the sweetest looking tabby knows just how fearsome and unforgiving felines can be when riled. It's not surprising then that when the Irish wanted to curse somebody or something they would invoke feline ferocity. Perhaps the most direct and powerful of these curses is "mallacht mo chait ort" (moll-oct muh hhot earth) or "the curse of my cat on you." This recognizes the power of cats and their penchant for anger and spite, and, more specifically, invokes the ancient superstitious belief that cats had magical powers— including the ability to curse their foes. Another more vivid example of a cat curse is the infernal invocation, wishing that *Go n-ithe an cat thú is go n-ithe an diabhal an cat* (guh nih hah an cot who iss go nih hah on jowl who) which translates as "may the cat eat you, and may the devil eat the cat." We'd say that this one is a recipe for indigestion all around (who wants to end up a hairball within a hairball)! However, in all good conscience I must implore you to deploy these kitty-cat curses with care. I don't want to get sued for the consequences!

Black Bog Cats

If, in the course of your stay in Ireland, you find yourself wandering into a gift shop, you're likely to come across items featuring the likeness of a black bog cat. These figurines or lucky charms originate from legendary large black cats that prowled the shores of Loch Neagh. Such oversized kitties munched away on the fauna around the lake—insects, little rodents and whatever else took their fancy. Those who happened upon this apparition were generally bestowed with good luck. Therefore, if you acquire these charms on your journey (or perhaps closer to home at your local friendly Irish gift shop) they should bring you the same good fortune. At least that's how the story goes. And who can tell better stories than the Irish themselves?

Maelduinn and the Malicious Moggy

Maelduinn was a handsome young man whose biological father was killed by robbers yet was lucky enough to get himself adopted by an Irish queen. It's a complex tale so bear with me! To avenge his father's death, Maelduinn set out on a sea voyage in a small boat. After many adventures, he and his fearless crew reached a compact island with a white fortification on it. Around the fort were many white houses. Maelduinn and his companions entered the finest dwelling they came across. Inside they found a wee cat amusing himself by jumping from one column to another, glancing at the newcomers but not stopping his play. Soon, the adventurers noticed that there were rows of magnificent jewelry and swords of gold and silver strewn about the place. In the center of the house lay a sumptuous feast that included a succulent roasted ox and ample supplies of liquor. Maelduinn asked the cat if it was okay to partake of the victuals and the cat (in typical cat-like fashion) ignored him. Then, as one of Maelduinn's foster brothers hastily grabbed one of the gorgeous gold necklaces, Maelduinn motioned towards the cat and warned his brother against the move. Undeterred, Maelduinn's foolish foster brother started to walk away with the priceless golden collar. As the foster brother made to leave, the cat jumped from a pillar darting through the brother "like a fiery arrow," burning the thief to a crispy pile of ashes. The cat then sauntered back to his spot on the pillar. Keeping his composure, Maelduinn returned the precious jewelry to its rightful place, uttered repentant words to the cat, and gathered up his brother's ashes. After throwing the dusty remains into the sea, he and his remaining crew high-tailed it off the island as soon as possible. The moral of the story, we presume, is to beware of cats guarding precious treasure. Maybe Cartier could benefit from hiring some Irish cats as store detectives!

Black Cats and Shipwrecks

When Oscar the black cat died at an old sailor's home in Belfast, Northern Ireland, you might be forgiven for supposing there was nothing unusual about the passing of one modest little member of felinekind. Yet, this unassuming cat had a long and most unique marine career behind him. You see, the remarkable Oscar had used up quite a few of his lives escaping from sinking ships. First, this kitty found himself aboard the Bismarck, a German battleship charged with attacking Allied ships as they brought supplies across the North Atlantic sea route during World War Two. Desperate to eliminate the threat posed by The Bismarck, the Allies attacked and eventually sank it. However, lucky cat Oscar narrowly escaped a watery grave when the British vessel, HMS Cossack plucked the knackered tabby from the sea. Amazed at the cat's survival skills, his new crew named him Unsinkable Sam. Apparently unsatisfied with his new home, Sam escaped yet again and chose a new home aboard the British HMS Ark Royal. However, while Sam had proved himself unsinkable, the boat beneath his wee paws wasn't so buoyant. Less than a month later that vessel was in turn torpedoed and sank. Uncannily, the lucky kitty escaped drowning and this time it was the crew of the British ship HMS Legion who scooped him out of the water. After that, Oscar, AKA Sam the Unsinkable's, seafaring days were over. He spent the rest of his existence on dry land—purring like a steam engine in the Emerald Isle. We're pretty confident that the navy was glad to not attract any more lousy luck from Oscar's presence.

Listening for the Fairies

Ever get the feeling that your kooky cat can hear the music of the fairy folk as they dance away the wee hours of the morning? Well, anything's possible... You see, it's said that the famous mystical melody from the other world is notoriously hard to hear. However, cats have a far more acute sense of hearing than we do. For instance, they can hear tones 1.5 octaves higher than humans can. In addition, they can quickly rotate their adorable ears to determine precisely where a sound is emanating from. This ability to swivel their ears is attributable to a remarkable 27 muscles that control each ear. So, if your puss gets a dreamy, far-away look on his face and his ears twitch, fairy music could well be the cause.

The Mysterious Cat-Like Rock Formation

Cats, cats everywhere. We're talking not just about the real life physical felines that provide us humans with such pleasant companionship. No, we refer instead to that phenomenon of when you see things that resemble a cat. So, you stop, you glance again, and then you realize that it's been nothing more than a trick of the eye. That lump under the blankets, that rustle in the bush was not in fact a cat but a figment of your imagination. This phenomenon could explain the mysterious rock formation at the Hill of Uisneach, in County Westmeath. From this ancient sacred site, they say you can see up to twenty counties on a clear day. The sacredness of the location was largely due to the fact that it is the burial place of Eriu, the ancient goddess after whom the island of Erin is named. And Erin, as we know, is the ancient name for Ireland. Eriu's resting place is marked by two remarkable stones which resemble a cat chasing a mouse. Whether the stones were designed to represent such a playful image or whether it's wishful thinking that they do we're not quite sure. Perhaps that's just another Irish mystery that will never be solved.

The Black Cat of Killakee House

In the fair county of Wicklow can be found a dwelling place known as Killakee house. In the late 1960s, the O'Brien family decided to upgrade the then rather decrepit structure into an arts center and tearoom. During the renovations, a team of painters lodged at the house so that the work could be completed speedily. They reported strange goings on, including seeing a black cat the size of a large dog! Initially, the owners dismissed the painters' accounts as delusions, tall tales inspired by a bit of nighttime tipple or the result of tricks played by local mischief-makers. However, in 1970, the respected national newspaper, *The Irish Independent*, reported that Mrs. O'Brien could not sleep in the house because of the weird howling of her terrified dogs who seemed to sense something nefarious afoot. Also, some mysterious force had caused quite a bit of destruction inside the house, even though a careful investigation uncovered no evidence that any human invaders had broken in. Subsequently, two artists at the house saw a black cat and then the apparition of a three-foot-high man who transformed himself into a cat. Later that decade, the owners exorcised the house, and as far as the occupants could gather at that time, the ghostly cats were gone for good. Nonetheless, more recent reports claim that there may have been other spooky occurrences since then. Who knows, it could be another phantom cat creeping around the place? I certainly wouldn't spend a night at Kilakee House, would you?

The Irish Cat Kings

Anyone fond of cats can't contest that there's a regal bearing about them. Graceful, elegant, and inclined to look down upon their human servants from the nearest elevated perch, it's no wonder the ancient Egyptians chose these imperious animals as an object of worship. But the pyramids weren't the only historical home to feline royalty. Once you're done perusing the history of Egyptian cat gods, you may like to turn your attention to the intriguing tale of the Irish cat kings. These magical cats were known in the Gaelic tongue as *cait sidhe* (pronounced as caught shee), which can be translated as fairy or spirit cats. In appearance, these conventional-seeming kitties were ordinary enough, taking the form of a large-ish black cat with a blaze of white fur on its chest. But despite their unassuming form, these creatures were not to be trifled with. Tradition held that on Samhain, the feast on which

Halloween is based, the supernatural and the normal worlds overlapped. On this night, there were more of the *cait sidhe* about and the custom was to leave out a saucer of milk for these otherworldly creatures, to ensure good luck in the year to come. Woe betide those foolish, stingy folks who didn't observe this custom for bad fortune would follow them--sometimes leading to their cows stopping milk production and reducing the farming family to financial ruin. However, those who were kind to the *cait sidhe* could expect gratitude and generosity in return. Witness the tale of the old lady, who on a wintry night, welcomed a black cat and its two kittens into her house, giving the feline family a saucer of milk by the fire. The mother cat did more than just meow. She spoke, thanking the woman for her kindness before all three cats vanished up the chimney, leaving in their wake more silver than the old woman could have earned in a month. Well, don't say we haven't given you the heads up. If you're ever in Ireland, be sure to be extra kind to any black cat with a white patch on its chest. After all, who couldn't use a boost to the family budget from a paranormal pussy cat?

Kitties At The Heart of Their Domain

Castle Cats

Now, while you might reasonably picture Irish cats as snuggling down in a barn somewhere or dozing contentedly by a cottage fire, there are other far grander residences that Irish cats inhabit. Imagine if you will the cat who is not just haughty in demeanor but is literally the king or queen of the castle. Ireland has a rich heritage of castles which dot the verdant countryside. On the Emerald Isle you can find many sorts of such fortified dwellings: ruined castles, Old Irish castles, Norman castles, even Victorian country houses built in the style of the castles of yore. Whatever their exact type, these are imposing structures worthy of your attention. Also deserving of note are those high and mighty felines who patrol the battlements and towers of Ireland's mighty castles. These castle kitties are of all breeds and their personalities are as unique as the mighty residences they inhabit. Take for example Gregan's Castle near Ballyvaughan in County Clare, whose cat custodian is a lovely white cat with black markings, and who goes by the name of Shelley. Bunratty Castle and its surrounding folk park village is home to some cats who alternate between sleeping in nooks in the castle and bedding down in cozy spots in the surrounding, more humble cottages. Let's not overlook Manderley Castle in South County Dublin, home of the enigmatic singer Enya who's said to have approximately a dozen cats sharing her stately home.

Brewery and Distillery Cats

Few observant individuals would dispute the crucial role that alcohol plays at the heart of Irish life. Drinking is not just a mere act here, it's a ritual. Some might even say that imbibing is something akin to a religion! Those of us who believe, as perhaps most of us reading this book do, that cats have a paw in just about everything important in our lives will not be at all surprised to know of the connection of Irish cats to the drinking culture. You see, two of the most essential and world-renowned institutions in Irish drinking life have cleverly kept Irish cats on their payroll. The function of these intrepid critters was to keep rodents away from the grain. The institutions we're speaking of are whiskey distillers Jameson and the world-famous purveyor of many a fine pint of stout, the Guinness brewery. Historians have discovered evidence that cats were kept on the payroll in both companies. Yes, you've got that right: Irish kitties guarded the grain that made the alcohol that fueled the craic that has made this mighty little island famous right up to the present day. These cats were perhaps the most valued employees in the country in their day, even if most folk weren't aware of their existence. We're glad that we have uncovered this story so that the respect and interest due these special felines can be made in the proper manner.

Five-Star Cat Hotel

Your friends or family might tease you that your cat's usual surroundings and general level of treatment equal that of any five-star hotel or resort across the globe. However, now you actually can treat you and your dear pet to a truly pampered experience at one of Ireland's top resorts: the lavish Ashford Castle hotel, situated in the West of Ireland in County Mayo. Here amidst the magnificent grounds, you and Fluffy can indulge every whim as you luxuriate in one of the world's most renowned hostelries. Such a decadent indulgence will set you back a relatively modest sum of €40 per night to bring kitty along with you. Please note that a room for you will cost several hundred euro, possibly the only time cat lovers will spend more on themselves than on their cat! In addition, Ashford Castle's management will ask you to pay a refundable €1000 damage deposit that will be reimbursed to you at the end of your stay—provided that neither you nor kitty go on a scratch, tear, and biting rampage. But we know that neither of you would ever dream of such a thing…

Irish Pub Cats

If you're familiar with a single cat-based saying, it's probably "curiosity killed the cat." If you're familiar with any cat, you know that's an apt warning for these investigative animals. If your cat is of a particularly inquisitive nature, the best place for any knowledge-gathering mission in an Irish village would be none other than the local Irish pub. Here, you and your cats are likely to hear everything from the latest disputes about cows wandering from one farmer's land to who in town bakes the absolute best Irish soda bread. The pub itself may very well have a cat in residence. Imagine what a sublime existence this would be for a cat of the right temperament and disposition. Just visualize all the attention from the steady stream of imbibers and revelers. We're confident that many cats might apply for such a position, however only a few would be chosen. Among the fortunate is the lucky Goshken who lives in McCarthy's pub in Dingle, County Kerry. This distinguished fellow oversees the evening's proceedings with an air of regal superiority. He'll sometimes deign to socialize, making his way imperiously through the crowd when he feels like it, and if you're very lucky, hop in your booth and keep you company while you down your pint. Maybe one day we'll make a trip to see dear old Goshken. We hope you'll join us. Of course, we'll toast each other with a hearty *sláinte!* That's "to your good health" in the Irish tongue.

The Female of the Species

Cats have long been associated with the female sphere of influence. The Latin for cat is the feminine noun *felis*. In Medieval times, Irish laws referred to hounds being suitable for men while small dogs and cats were deemed appropriate for ladyfolk (the text mentions that such cats may be kept on pillows). In pre-feminist times, various sources reproached women as being vain, impetuous, unreliable, and impulsive, traits commonly associated with kitties as well. Worst of all, authorities saw both cats and women as resistant to the rules and order associated with masculinity. Just try and tell a cat what to do and at best you'll get ignored. At worst, you'll earn a claw-filled swipe and really, you'd probably only have yourself to blame. It seemed only natural to the pre-modern mind that being so alike there would be a natural kinship between women and cats. So, it's not at all surprising that women and cats were often featured together in the art of the period.

Cream for Table Two!

Mealtime rituals vary in Irish cat-run households, yet most observe separate dining spaces, with kitty supping from a bowl on the floor and humankind enjoying their repast with a knife and fork, table, and chair. Still, you must admit that dinner at home every night can get boring for you—and—for Fluffy. However, if you and your kitty companion find yourselves in Ireland, and you'd prefer supper out on the town—at least once in a while—you're in luck! You see, bringing your cat to an Irish restaurant is legally okay—at the establishment's discretion. Yes, you heard it right. A rule banning cats and dogs from restaurants which was enacted in the 1950s has now been overturned. So, you and kitty can now share a meal—perhaps have some liver pate to start, followed by catnip roast chicken and a bowl of cream to finish. Just one thing—food prep and storage areas are still off limits so watch that your feline companion doesn't wander too far from the table or you'll both end up in trouble.

Cats and the Church

St. Gertrude's Day—St. Patrick's Day for Cats

Now, you've probably never wondered how cats spend Saint Patrick's Day. If asked, you might guess they try to avoid at all costs being dressed up in miniature Aran sweaters draped with green beads and being made to wear silly green hats and other headgear. Besides, it's safe to assume that they'd rather steer clear of the noisy hordes who maraud around the parish drinking, carousing, and carrying on. Well, it might surprise you to learn that on Saint Patrick's Day Irish cats could be offering up a quietly meowed prayer to a Belgian saint by the name of Gertrude. You see, March 17th is not only the feast day of Saint Patrick, the beloved patron of the Emerald Isle, but it is also the feast day of Saint Gertrude. It's not known why Gertrude is the patron saint of cats, however some writings show that she and her fellow devout nuns kept some feline companions to ward off mice and rats in the convent where they lived during the 13th century. Paintings depict Saint Gertrude with the cat by her side and mice in the background. Perhaps cats and the holy woman worked alongside each other. Saint Gertrude presumably occupied herself with prayer and good works, and her companion cats toiled to keep those pesky rodents at bay. Together they ensured that there would be enough food to last through lean times of famine and general shortage—a critical task in the days before refrigeration and other advanced food preservation techniques. So, this year, when March 17th rolls around be sure not only to bid your friends and neighbors a happy Saint Patrick's Day but also take a moment to wish your furry friends a joyful and prayerful feast of Saint Gertrude.

The Organist's Cat

Some cats love music and will listen intently to their favorite genre. And most cats are curious and love to chase rodents. We're not sure which category the next curious kitty falls into. All we'll say is this poor cat reached the end of his nine lives. Our tragic tale takes place in Christ Church Cathedral in Dublin town. There has been a religious presence on this site since Viking times. On display in the crypt alongside a renowned collection of silver chalices, candlesticks, and the heart of Saint Lawrence O'Toole are the mummified remains of a cat and a rat. Both hunter and prey were found in the 1850s in the pipe of an organ. It seems the foolish feline chased the rat into the organ—and both got stuck—for all eternity! So odd and striking are the pair that James Joyce uses them in literature as a simile for somebody who was strongly connected to somebody else.

An Aquatic Terror

The Irish saints traveled far and wide in their quest to spread Christianity. None, however, went farther away or left more fantastical accounts of his travels than St. Brendan. Some even think Brendan may have reached America several centuries before Columbus. On one of these forays, St. Brendan and his fellow monks came upon a lovely island with a whirlpool full of easy-to-catch fish. Living on the island in a stone church was a frail old monk who approached St. Brendan warning him of a sea cat who was a danger to their lives. The holy man explained that originally, the monstrous cat had been an itty-bitty kitty whom the monks had fed with fish but that over time, the wee moggie developed an enormous size and an equally huge attitude problem. St. Brendan and his monks hightailed it off the island, only to find themselves pursued by a vast sea cat swimming after their boat. They prayed to God for deliverance and the Lord saw fit to send another sea monster who killed the terrifying tabby. The moral of the story: Don't overfeed your cat or it will turn into an aquatic terror!

The Pope's Kitten

Any true lover of cats likely remembers longing for a kitten as a child. I bet you can still feel the excitement as you pictured your furry new companion. Oh, the games you'd play and the *craic* (Irish for high jinks) you'd have. Well, one little Irish girl was promised a kitten under rather public circumstances. On Pope Francis's visit to Ireland in 2018, the Irish Minister for Foreign Affairs, Simon Coveney, was to greet the Pope at Dublin Airport. Alongside him were his wife and three daughters: Annalise (5), Jessica (7) and Beth (9). Annalise was to present his Holiness with flowers. However, at the last minute, she got cold feet. So, the parental bribery began. Annalise was offered in turn (and declined each time) a fancy meal, use of her Dad's phone for a month, or a gift of his iPad. Sensing he had a crisis on his hand, Mr. Coveney made his most enticing offer, that of a kitten. The pragmatic little Annalise agreed immediately, and the greeting ceremony went ahead without a hitch. We're told that Annalise's kittenly reward was a black rescue who had innocently crawled into a warm car engine for forty winks; when the car engine was turned on he had nearly died. Despite being nursed carefully back to health, the kitten had lost an ear. Named

"Spirit" (presumably both for his plucky bravery and the religious associations with the Pope's visit), this one-eared kitten is now the lucky recipient of one little Irish girl's undying affection.

Literary Felines

Cat Poetry

In 1923, W. B. Yeats won the Nobel Prize for literature and this Irish man of letters is recognized as perhaps one of the finest poets ever to roam the earth. One of his most charming poems is *The Cat and the Moon*. In this delightful composition, Yeats says that the moon could learn a thing or two from the cat in terms of grace and its refined dance. There is a contrast between the two, with the cat being black and the moon white, yet one sees they exist together in a kind of symbiosis. It's interesting also to note that the moon and the cat both come to life at night. Whatever the undoubted merits of its finer linguistic details we think this is a charming composition that pays worthy tribute to the cat's inherent elegance.

James Joyce, Samuel Beckett, and Their Cats

The famed Irish scribes James Joyce and Samuel Beckett had even more in common than one might think. As many an Irish schoolchild learns, both these men came originally from Dublin and both left their home countries and spent considerable time in Paris. Also, they had a shared desire to escape the stifling restrictions of a distinctly conservative and overbearingly religious society. What you may not know is that a common love of cats bound them together. Beckett was photographed on quite a few occasions with his beloved cats, their devotion to each other being clear from the pose and attitude which he and the cats assumed in the photographs. James Joyce was also a dedicated lover of cats and his work demonstrates this. For example, the very first conversation in his masterwork "Ulysses" is a conversation between the protagonist Leopold Bloom, who was a kind-hearted soul, and a hungry cat. What is less well known are the series of letters that Joyce wrote to his grandson Steven in which he told stories about cats. These tabby tales were later published as *The Cat and the Devil* and *The Cats of Copenhagen*. In these whimsical and delightful stories, the sheer delight that grandfather and grandson find in feline companionship is clearly evident. There is not so much evidence in Beckett's work of his love for cats, but who is to say that *Waiting for Godot* with its three main protagonists in garbage cans may not have had some connection to alley cats? This hypothesis is a new theory I've just conjured up—a controversial one—and we're just throwing it out there. Nonetheless, we've come across a series of amusing posters online featuring cats and quotes from Beckett so maybe we're not the only ones convinced of a possible connection.

Literary Cat Ladies

We've all heard of cat ladies, those fine, fiercely independent women whose lives revolve around cats and everything cat related. Does that describe anybody reading this? Come on, let's be honest people! One subspecies of these feline inclined females is the literary cat lady of which Ireland (renowned for its writers) has an abundant supply. The premiere example would be Maeve Binchy, that beloved writer (alas, no longer with us) whose accessible yet thought-provoking novels have garnered worldwide fame. During her writing career, the kindly scribe shared her working space with her husband, the children's book writer Gordon Snell and with their cats: a white female called Audrey and a stately marmalade-and-white male called Fred. Imagine how many inspiring and well-crafted stories these two lucky kitties were witness to... Cats are indeed the ideal writer's companion, "guarding" piles of manuscripts, providing a welcome distraction when needed and not requiring walks as dogs would. Besides, there's something about a comforting purr that puts one in the zone and gets the creative juices flowing. So, if you're inspired to try your hand at writing, pull up a pussycat and get typing...

Oscar Wilde

"Cats are put on earth to remind us that not everything has a purpose."

—Oscar Wilde

One of Ireland's finest literary sons Oscar Wilde was a renowned lover of beauty. This flamboyant writer's appreciation for the sophisticated in all its forms is legendary. Therefore, it's no wonder he realized that cats need not necessarily have a mundane purpose for being on Earth and that they can legitimately claim a right to exist on this planet simply for the sake of their awe-inspiring beauty. Wilde's respect for felines was so great that on one occasion he saw a cat asleep on his treasured fur coat. Rather than wake the cat, he cut off the sleeve of the pricey garment. We salute somebody who would have so much consideration for a dozing kitty as to sacrifice one of his most valuable possessions. From such a lover of beauty and things that are often overlooked in the hurly burly of the modern world, we would expect nothing less. Wilde was the true cat lover to top all cat lovers.

Country Cousins

Bodacious the Shepherd Cat

In the realm of animal husbandry, our thoughts might first go to such loyal and energetic canine breeds as the border collie, its body a whir of color as it dashes across fields and up across steep dales to gather up the errant sheep. So, it might surprise you to know that Ireland was home to a shepherd cat, by the fierce name of none other than Bodacious. This gray cat with a shaggy coat—suited to the brisk outdoor life—spent over 11 years on the sheep farm of Suzanna Crampton. He followed her everywhere on her day-to-day rounds of the farmstead. Realizing how unique this "shepherd cat" was, Suzanna set up a Twitter account chronicling his unconventional life. The page grew to over 17,000 followers who gobbled up stories of Bodacious's antics. Eventually the interest in Bodacious grew so great he became the subject of a book published by HarperCollins all over the world. This entertaining tome chronicled all aspects of sheep farming, with Bodacious accompanying shepherd Suzanna as she did her rounds. Sadly, Bodacious is no longer with us, having passed away on February 1st, 2019. We have an inkling he is joyfully tending his flock in the great beyond.

Irish Catnip Farmers

County Offaly is the location of Ireland's first commercial catnip grower. The business is called Fred's Catnip Farm. Owner Aideen Day was dismayed at the quality of catnip *(nepeta cataria)* that she found when seeking a treat for her beloved cat Fred. So, enterprising soul that she is, she decided to order some seeds online. The crop she grew so enamored fluffy Fred that she thought maybe other cats would enjoy such a tantalizing treat. Hence the birth of Fred's Catnip Farm. Catnip, as we all know, has an exhilarating effect on cats of all sizes. You can search online for adorable videos of even the largest of the *Felidae* family like lions and tigers (oh my!) reacting to its mind-altering delights. However, the active ingredient nepetalactone only works on approximately 50% of cats. The results vary from feline to feline. However, a period of exuberance, shenanigans and general high jinks are all part of the mellow experience, which is said to resemble the effect of marijuana on humans. We're certain that Ireland's mouse-chasing inhabitants are twitching their tails to have Ireland's first catnip farm in their midst. Certain lucky local cats are likely to break in and take a well-deserved little "trip" amid those lush and lovely green Irish fields! However, don't bother enticing the tiniest fuzzballs with this trippy herb. Young kittens won't care, as the response to catnip doesn't appear until cats are at least three months old.

Cats in Art

Philatelic Felines

Nothing says you've arrived like a "stamp of approval." In 2007, the Irish Post Office issued its very first postage stamps to feature cats. About time, we'd say! What took them so long? They should have been the first animal stamps issued… Critters featured before then included beetles, dogs, and other creatures. These milestone philatelic wonders were comic in style and featured the work of political cartoonist Martin Turner, done in sarcastic style and including a pair of "Cool Cats." Another set of popular stamps, released in 2014, featured photographs of four pedigree cats: Persian, Maine Coon, Siamese, and Burmese. These postal tributes reflected the fact that cats are now Ireland's most popular pet. These stamps were also intended to raise awareness of animal welfare issues.

The Sculpted Cat with Two Tails

In County Tipperary there are several carvings showing a cat with two tails. Well, apart from being able to swat away twice as many flies and providing the fastidious feline with more fur to brush, we were rather curious to know what this strange two-tailed representation could mean. It turns out these two tailed tabbies seem to tie back to the so-called *Goban Saor*. While Ireland's many churches and monasteries were being constructed, roving bands of masons and carvers would roam the countryside living in tents as they plied their trade for weeks, months or even years at a particular site. Now, these men lived outside the rules of conventional society, being itinerants as they were. They were also known as a rather secretive bunch. There is a legend that in the seventh century one particular stonemason, known to history as the *Goban Saor*, was asked to prove his skill by the abbot of a monastery by carving a sculpture overnight, of a cat with two tails. The obnoxious abbot who had asked him to complete such a task was certain the mason (the *Goban Saor)* could not comply. It surprised the odious taskmaster to return the next morning and find the sculpture complete (a miraculous feat in such a short time). Meanwhile the sculptor had vanished. Proud of the legendary mason's carving skills, other stone masons took to carving this mysterious symbol of the cat with two tails on various hidden nooks and crannies on buildings around County Tipperary. Paying tribute to the story, a contemporary sculptor by the name of David Gorey is strongly influenced by the *Goban Saor*, and the cat with two tails, and incorporates these motifs into his own work.

Cat-Themed Ornaments

Domestic cats sleep an average of twelve to sixteen hours a day. When your sweet little kitty is curled up and snoozing, perhaps enjoying dreams of milk and mice as far as the eye can see, it may be easy to forget what a naughty little agent of chaos she can be when the spirit moves her. One need only watch a fully awake cat stalking your shelves, knocking knick-knacks to the ground, or swatting your mug of tea right off the edge of the table. Is there anything cats enjoy more than such mischief? If you've ever tried to share a home with a tabby as well as a decorated Christmas tree, you've likely seen that for kitty, your Tannenbaum is too tempting by half.

But if you are a brave enough soul to introduce delicate ornaments into a space occupied by a naughty moggie or two (or if you're currently cat-less), may we suggest cat themed ornaments from two classic Irish purveyors of decorative delights. For over a hundred and thirty years, Belleek Pottery Ltd in Belleek, County Fermanagh has produced porcelain famous the world over. Delicate and thin, with a slight iridescent sheen, this fine china is prized for many uses. If you can keep it out of paws-reach, consider their adorable 'Quizzical Cat' ornament, complete with a sly grin and a jaunty shamrock collar.

If your fuzzy friend loves spending their days lazing by the nearest heat source, perhaps getting in touch with an ancestral memory of the days when peat from the local bog blazed bright in the hearth, consider Island Turf Crafts. Located in Northern Ireland these creative folks fashion jewelry, decorations, and other ornamental objects from authentic Irish peat turf. While not unbreakable, their Lucky Black Bog Cat ornament is a bit sturdier than the kitty collectibles one might order from Belleek, and it sports an adorably smug little smile. Both of these feline fripperies can be found on the websites for these fine Irish establishments, and if you reside outside the Emerald Isle, you're in luck, because both of these companies ship worldwide. How you keep these ornaments safe from feline harm once they arrive on your doorstep is up to you.

Some Feline Facts and Figures

Color-Blind Cats and Forty Shades of Green

Cats are generally considered colorblind. That is to say they see this colorful world of ours in tones of black, gray, and white, almost as if they were watching a black-and-white movie. However, this oversimplification is not the full extent of the story. Far from it. It's fortunate for Ireland's kitties that apart from mainly seeing things in shades of gray they also can sense various hues of the colors green and blue. This ability means they can experience and enjoy Ireland's legendary forty shades of green. Otherwise, what a shame it would be for them to miss the natural verdant splendor that surrounds them on this famously emerald isle. The blue they perceive can also be useful for admiring Ireland's storm-tossed seas. It might also be useful for spotting the occasional patch of blue that peeks through the great tumultuous clouds sweeping in from the Atlantic.

What Color is an Irish Cat?

If you try to conjure up an Irish cat in your mind's eye, we wonder what form he or she might take. Would it perhaps be a gray tabby? Could it be a cozy little orange mite? Well, the answer, in fact, according to a 2015 survey is that in reality, it's far more likely to be a black cat with patches of white, for the study showed that this is, in fact, the most common kitty color type across the island of Ireland. Mixed in with the myriad of moggies of various colors, you can find a certain number of tortoiseshells. Irish folklore tells us that tortoiseshell cats bring good fortune. In fact, there's also the folk tradition that passing a tortoiseshell cat's tail over a wart will get rid of the pesky skin affliction! This strategy

72

is a remedy worth trying if you have that dermatological complaint and know any tortoiseshells. If you can avoid the likely swipe of the indignant fuzzball's claws, it'd certainly be cheaper than a visit to a boring old human dermatologist…

Dublin's Cat Fair

Starting in 2018, the Dublin cat fair has quickly become a fixture on the calendar of cat lovers across the country. But contrary to what a reasonable friend of felines might surmise, there are in fact no actual kitty cats present at this festival. Nor is it a free-for-all like the infamous Donnybrook fair of yore. Neither is it a place to buy and sell cats as might be the case in a country marketplace, which would also be called a fair. It turns out this cat fair is a forum for organizations, individuals, and companies related to the cat world to get together, to exchange information and to bond over their combined love of cats and all things feline. It's grown in size year on year and the progress shows no signs of abating. It's an interesting event and who knows, if you find yourself in the area during November it might be worth your time to drop in and just while away a couple of hours in the company of fellow cat lovers. We expect that it will continue to flourish. We wish this enterprise all the luck in the world or, even better, all the luck of the Irish!

Quirky Cats

Mama Cat and Her Ducklings

There have been some extraordinary tales of cats mothering other species. In fact, this maternal instinct seems to be rather strong towards cute little creatures just after the mama cat has given birth and her mothering hormones are still surging. In Clara, County Offaly, in 2013, for example, a striped, gray tabby with white markings, the pet of Ronan and Emma Lalley, mothered three little ducklings! The owners thought the ducklings had gone missing and feared that the cats may have had the poor little quackers for lunch. Imagine their surprise when they found the tiny ducklings snuggled soundly up against their new cat mama. It just goes to show that the laws of nature aren't inflexible and that animals of different species can, in fact, co-exist in harmony. Not only that—they can become the best of buddies. Who would have thought?

Kitty Paying His Last Respects

Funerals have a special place in Irish culture. It's a time for the whole community to come together to pay respects to the departed, to exchange news and information, and to meditate on the inevitable passing of time, as well as the cycles of life and death. If you have any respect, affection, or connection that goes beyond the casual with the deceased, you will be sure to attend their funeral. Yet, inhabitants of Castlemane, Co. Kerry were somewhat taken aback to note an unaccompanied tortoiseshell cat at a local burial in 2014. The deceased was a known cat lover. It seems the grieving creature had made its way there under the hood of a car. The presence of this tortoiseshell feline

was remarkable both for its solemnity and dignity in paying its respects; it sat still for the entire ceremony. This heart-rending tribute has to be one of the most incredible stories we've ever heard about Irish cats. We can only assume that the deceased must have been exceptionally kind to the grief-stricken kitty.

Modern-Day Moggies

Moving to Ireland with Your Cat

If you're a fan of Ireland and all things Irish, we're sure you have at least daydreamed about moving to Ireland at some stage. And why not? It makes purrfect sense, as apart from the light-hearted bonhomie of the local population there is an abundance of beautiful landscape to behold in the country itself. Furthermore, this storied land now boasts an excellent infrastructure and an array of employment opportunities in various tech and other related fields. But of course, there's your beloved fur baby to consider: you wouldn't dream of leaving him or her at home while you enjoy your Irish adventure, would you?

Luckily, there's no need to say farewell to puss since Ireland has a straightforward and defined set of regulations for bringing pets across its border. If you're traveling from another European Union country, you'll need a pet passport. Yes, European pets have passports, and this precious little document will provide the fine folks at customs with all the information that shows it's OK for an animal to enter the country. However, if you're coming from a non-European point of departure such as the United States or Canada, you need to get a certificate testifying to the following: that your cat has been implanted with a microchip; and that your cat has been vaccinated against rabies. If someone asks whether kitty is traveling for business or pleasure, make sure to answer the latter, since you are required to attest that your cat is being moved for non-commercial purposes. Once you have your certificate in hand you'll need to make your travel arrangements, then it's a case of talking to the individual airlines about their travel requirements as these vary from carrier to carrier. Cats can be skittish creatures under even the best of circumstances, so be sure to pack some of your cat's most precious toys and a bit of familiar scented bedding, to ease the nerves of your feline flyer. We're sure she will settle in eventually, but there may be a period of adjustment when everyday items or objects from home may provide that extra sense of reassurance.

Cat Café

A cat café is one of those charming ideas that seem to us the very height of civilization. As well as providing gainful employment for otherwise indolent kitties, it also satisfies humans' deepest instincts to snuggle up with a furry heap of loveliness. So, it was with great delight that in October 2017, we learned of the opening of Dublin's very first cat lounge in the Smithfield area of the city. We assume that for a time it provided some sustenance and companionship to many delighted customers. However, on August 31, 2018, it unfortunately closed its doors. On occasion, even the best business ideas are ahead of their time. Or it could simply be a case of the stars not aligning. Whatever the situation with this worthwhile business venture, we salute the trail-blazing owner Georgina O'Neill who brought this incredible cat concept to Ireland. Who knows—and we're crossing our fingers this will be the case—perhaps one day she (or another cat-loving entrepreneur) will be able to reestablish this worthwhile endeavor?

Ireland's Very Own Pet Detective

Did your cat eat the sirloin steak left on the counter? Which of your kitties scratched the new sofa? Which end of your delicate princess did that puddle come from? These are all questions a curious cat owner might want answers to. However, it's riddles and puzzles of another ilk that preoccupy Ireland's premier pet detective. Dublin-based Robert Kenny is a Missing Animal Response Technician, and his mission is to recover lost cats and dogs. His valuable work takes him all over Ireland, throughout the UK as well as other parts of Europe. Since 2007 his company has retrieved about 4,500 cats and dogs. In a BBC interview, he stated that the rate of cat recovery is approximately 70%. He is aided in his rescue of missing cats by his gun dog Ace, named after none other than that famous pet detective, Ace Ventura.

The Celtic Tiger and Big Cats

Keeping a kitty in one's home is a source of great joy and immense satisfaction. That much is clear to any cat lover astute enough to pick up this humble book. Your furry friend sometimes seems like a wild creature, only just barely tamed by the prospect of a sunny patch of carpet or civilized by a bowl full of wet food (and perhaps the occasional scratch behind the ears). Yet there is an important distinction between the wildness of the average domesticated moggie (fierce huntress of houseflies though she may be) and the wildness of *actual* wild big cats. Some foolhardy Irishmen have learned there is in fact a legal distinction, when it was discovered they were in possession of some seriously big cats. And we're not talking about a portly Maine Coon here...

No, in this case, it was discovered that someone in Dublin was keeping an adult jaguar (named Princess!) as well as African serval cats in their garage of all places. The poor pussies were rescued and transported to the Dublin Zoo for safe keeping, while their fates were decided. Folks who want to keep such wild felines often have good intentions, said authorities, but these beasts aren't suited for suburban life. Some folks collect them as status symbols, but people like the owners of the menagerie found at Castlemahon, Co. Limerick (including two full-grown Siberian tigers and two tiger cubs) are tempting fate.

If you've ever been on the receiving end of a testy swipe from your sweet seven-pound tabby, you know a fierce hunter resides in even the smallest bit of feline fluff. One can only imagine the havoc that could be wrought by a five-hundred-pound tiger prowling a cul-de-sac in search of tasty human snacks. The tigers in Castlemahon were lucky enough to be relocated to a California Zoo before they made a meal of their owners, but don't think you'll be so lucky! Instead, it's the wisest course of action to stick to the more petite, domesticated-ish, and "legal" kitties to be found at your local humane society, and enjoy a taste of the wild that (probably) won't eat you alive.

The Disappearing Marmalade Cat

Anyone familiar with Irish eating habits will tell you that the Irish are partial to a slice or two of toast in the morning as part of their hearty Irish breakfast. On this crunchy morsel, they are likely to slather a generous helping of Ireland's luscious butter. Many of us also enjoy an ample dollop of marmalade, and one of the most popular brands on the

The Cats Of Ireland

market is Lamb Brothers' Old Time Irish marmalade, renowned for its golden color and generous chunks of delicious orange peel. On the label you can find a typical Irish fireside scene complete with a blazing peat fire, cozy armchairs and a wee black cat who has planted himself right by the radiant heat emanating from the fireplace. This cat has long been part of Ireland's culture. Teachers used to warn their students against being as lazy "as the cat on the Old Time Irish marmalade label." Well, we're shocked to tell you that at a dark moment in the 1970s the cat was removed from the label in the name of design improvement. You know, the kind of upgrade that manufacturers undertake from time to time to keep their products looking fresh and desirable in the marketplace. The reaction—as one might expect—was far from positive. Indignant consumers launched a national campaign to bring back the famous little cat to the marmalade label. Luckily, their collective effort was successful. The manufacturers restored Puss to a place of honor by the fire, a position from which he has never since strayed.

Puss and the Government Security Breach

In 2017, a kindly pensioner's acts of devotion toward three stray cats led to somewhat of a political crisis in Northern Ireland. Although Ms. Edna Watters had been feeding cats such as Ginger, Maggie, and Fury on the grounds of the Northern Irish government buildings for close to 30 years, an order had been issued demanding that she cease, as her presence (and that of the cats as well) was a supposed security risk. Despite the fact that the biggest threat presented by most kitties is the occasional hairball or knocked-over vase, *her* felines were now considered a security threat. Remarkably for a notoriously divided political landscape, all sides of the political spectrum united to condemn the heavy-handed security measure, eventually leaving the grateful moggies and their kind guardian in peace and allowing them to return to their beloved patch of ground.

Cat Cuddler Wanted

Any cat owner will tell you the visit to the vet can be a traumatic and trying experience for owner and fur baby alike. Most clever kitties seem to have a sixth sense that the cat carrier is not going to be used for a trip to a feline theme park or perhaps a venture to the latest chilled cream joint. So even before you head out the door with the kids, their nerves are already frazzled. Imagine then the scene when you arrive at the veterinarians to find the waiting room packed not only with strange cats but also with—horror of horrors—those most awful of creatures, big old mean dogs, or even little, tiny-teeny dogs, all of whose probably friendly barking seems threatening to nervous cats. Luckily, Just Cats Veterinary Clinic in Dublin has realized how stressful such a visit can be and has made their establishment a cats-only zone. No dogs allowed! Yet, even in this safe space, they realized that there was still a significant amount of stress involved. The supposed that this was the kind of nervous tension that a good old-fashioned snuggle could ease. That's why they decided to employ the services of a Cat Cuddler. The function of this incredible person is to pacify, and otherwise reassure, those nervous creatures who have come in for some veterinary care. So, Just Cats Veterinary Clinic advertised online for a suitable individual. Their posting went viral and applications poured in from around the world. What a wonderful and heartwarming story to show the love and respect in which the Irish hold their felines.

A Pedigree History

The Irish pedigree cat world comprises some dedicated groups of enthusiasts. The first formal cat-lovers' association to be founded in Ireland was none other than the Siamese cat club, formed in the post-war year of 1953. Initially, the club's focus, as you might reasonably suppose, was on felines of the Siamese persuasion. However, in 1968 the Governing Council of the Cat Fancy of Ireland (CGCFI) came into existence and took over all registrations of pedigree cats. As the new organization gained in strength, little by little, other breeds established a presence. There is now quite an extensive list of breeds represented. The varieties recognized are the same as those identified by the Governing Council of the Cat Fancy in England. Lest one accuse the CGCFI of pedigree snobbery their charter states that they are concerned with the wellbeing of *all* cats--whether they be pedigree or non-pedigree. Fair play to the CGFI!

The Future of Irish Cats

Throughout history the Irish have been known as a ferociously independent race. It's no wonder then that they might find a kindred spirit in the form of the fierce and scrappy cat. This connection between human and feline is one that's deeply interconnected. This bond is so deeply rooted that in Ireland cats have long found a sympathetic setting where they can live out their days in peace, harmony—and with an esteemed spot by a warm hearth. Now, lest you thought my theory about the innate similarities between *homo sapiens* and the *felis catus* who co-inhabit the Emerald Isle is tenuous, the pocket-sized cat compendium you've just read should provide you with some evidence for the deep and lasting ties that bind these two species together.

Irish humans and their cats do have so much in common… While neither take well to being told what to do, you will find they are both full of affection and warmth—but only under certain conditions. What are those terms you might ask? Well, both the Irish and their moggies will soon make these rules (or should that be 'guidelines'?) clear to you. Both man and beast co-inhabit a wind-tossed speck of land buffeted by wind and rain. Because this emerald landscape is rich agricultural domain, the destiny of both humans and mousers are interwoven with the timelines of planting, sowing, reaping, and harvesting, not to mention those of animal husbandry and its associated cycles.

As we've seen throughout this book, cats hold a special place in the Irish hearts and the Irish imagination, in its culture, and its legends. Cats have had an extraordinary influence on song, poetry, and books. And along the way, felines have provided plenty of entertainment and food for thought. This leads us to the question: What does the future hold for the cats of Ireland?

This is a fascinating question to ponder, and I'll try to answer it as best I can. On a practical note, cats are well suited to the modern human's work-heavy lifestyle since their civilized use of a litter box means they don't need to be walked. I believe that cats will only grow in popularity as Irish pets. A recent survey generated by Pedigree Ireland and Whiskas Ireland, shows that Irish people feel a special bond with their cats. We think that this exceptional connection that the Irish experience with their cats means our feline friends will always have a place at the center of Irish life.

About The Author

O riginally from Ireland, I'm a writer, editor and researcher based in New York. I'm always on the lookout for a special Irish gift whether for Christmas, birthdays, or just to say "Thanks."

A while back I happened to notice that as well as being fans of the Emerald Isle the majority of my friends are cat lovers. And, just about everyone I know is a devoted book enthusiast. Bearing all this in mind, off I set in search of an Irish-themed book on cats— as a gift for my friends who happen to be fond of felines. To my great surprise, I couldn't find anything that fit the bill. There were a couple of fun knick knacks, but not much in the way of the written word.

If my shamrock-loving, cat-hugging friends were to get the gift they deserved, there was no choice but to set about writing a book especially for them. "It couldn't be that hard…" I reckoned, "it should be relatively easy to research." Well, it took far longer than I expected. There was a snippet about an Irish cat in an old newspaper, a random mention of a notable feline in a folktale. Gradually, I pieced together what I hope is an entertaining collection that should tell you all you'd like to know about "The Cats of Ireland."

Other *B*ooks by *Séamus Mullarkey*

F*ck You I'm Irish: Why We Irish Are Awesome recounts in a lively, highly irreverent tone, exactly how a tiny, remote country--two-thirds the size of Maine, has had such an outsized impact on the entire world. It chronicles that fighting Irish spirit and how Ireland has played such an important role in global affairs. It's a great gift for an Irish birthday, Irish Christmas, and of course, the ideal Irish gift for St. Patrick's Day. Written by Séamus Mullarkey, under the pen name of Rashers Tierney, Séamus modestly states that this book sets out to be "the Irish gift to top all other Irish gifts." To purchase a copy, simply click the link or scan the code below…

https://amzn.to/2O21BIk

WHY NOT GET A **FREE E-BOOK** TO FIND OUT IF YOUR CAT MIGHT ACTUALLY BE IRISH…?

Making a connection with others around the world is the best part of writing. From time to time, I send emails with details of new releases, special offers, and other news related to books about Irish topics, cats, and to humor in general.

If you sign up for my mailing list today, I'll send you a wee e-book that outlines the twenty-five signs that your cat is Irish.

You can get this e-book **for free**! As a **special bonus** you'll **also** be able to get free copies of my future books—all just for giving your honest review! Simply use the link or scan the code below..

https://bit.ly/3kian13

ENJOYED THIS BOOK? *YOU* CAN MAKE A REAL DIFFERENCE.

Reviews are the most powerful tool when it comes to getting the word out about my books. I would love to be able to promote a book like the big publishing houses, but I'm just a one-man operation and can't take out full-page ads in the newspapers like they do.

However, I do have a treasured resource that these publishers would do anything to get their hands on.

A kind and loyal group of readers who aren't afraid to share the love...

Sincere, honest reviews that come from the heart bring my books to the attention of other readers, who will hopefully like them just as much.

If this book brought you a few moments of pleasure, I'd be forever grateful if you took just a few minutes out of your busy day to leave a review (don't worry if it's just a couple of words) on the book's Amazon page.

You can get to the review page simply by following the link below.

https://tinyurl.com/354wbynj

Credits for Illustrations

Signing my books

Photograph author's own

--Free for commercial use, no attribution required

Cats in History

https://pixabay.com/photos/cat-pet-animal-cute-mountains-2406101/

--Free for commercial use, no attribution required.

Glamourpusses

https://www.shutterstock.com/image-photo/domestic-medium-hair-cat-yellow-summer-1796101264

--Royalty-free stock photo ID: 1796101264—Used under license from shutterstock.

Adventurous Cats

https://commons.wikimedia.org/wiki/File:HMS_Vindex_ships_cat_WWI_IWM_Q_73724.jpg

--This work created by the United Kingdom Government is in the public domain.

Song, Story, and Verse

https://pixabay.com/illustrations/quartet-cat-violin-cello-viola-2536555/*Furballs in Folklore*

Country Cousins

https://pixabay.com/photos/barn-kitten-cat-feline-country-14188/

--Free for commercial use, no attribution required.

Cats in Art

https://www.shutterstock.com/image-photo/lilac-blotched-tabby-american-curl-cat-1043397298

--Used under license from shutterstock.

Some Feline Facts and Figures

https://pixabay.com/illustrations/vintage-kitten-school-kittens-cat-4178304/

--Free for commercial use, no attribution required.

Quirky Cats

https://commons.wikimedia.org/wiki/File:Cat_in_Bowl.jpg

--This work is in the public domain.

Modern-Day Moggies

https://commons.wikimedia.org/wiki/Category:Cats_with_computers#/media/File:Cat_on_laptop_-_Just_Browsing.jpg

--This file is licensed under the Creative Commons Attribution 2.0 Generic license. Author Wilson Afonso, Sydney, Australia. No changes made to the image.

The Future of Irish Cats

About the Author

Made in the USA
Middletown, DE
12 November 2021

52298861R00068